P9-CBM-016

¡Mírame, ahí voy! / Watch Me Go!

MI PATINETA
MY SCOOTER

Victor Blaine
Traducido por Eida de la Vega

PowerKiDS press.

New York

Published in 2015 by The Rosen Publishing Group, Inc.
29 East 21st Street, New York, NY 10010

First Edition

Editor: Sarah Machajewski
Book Design: Mickey Harmon
Spanish Translation: Eida de la Vega

Photo Credits: Cover, pp. 1, 21 Stephen Simpson/Taxi/Getty Images; p. 5 jambro/Shutterstock.com; p. 6 Frank Siteman/age fotostock/Getty Images; p. 9 © iStockphoto.com/donkeyru; p. 10 Szasz-Fabian Jozsef/Shutterstock.com; p. 13 Studio 37/Shutterstock.com; p. 14 © iStockphoto.com/jessicaphoto; pp. 17, 18 Stephen Simpson/Iconica/Getty Images; p. 22 Pavel L Photo and Video/Shutterstock.com.

Library of Congress Cataloging-in-Publication Data

Blaine, Victor.
My scooter = Mi patineta / by Victor Blaine.
p. cm. — (Watch me go! = ¡Mírame, ahí voy!)
Parallel title: ¡Mírame, ahí voy!.
In English and Spanish.
Includes index.
ISBN 978-1-4994-0288-9 (library binding)
1. Scootering — Juvenile literature. 2. Scooters — Juvenile literature. I. Title.
GV859.77 B53 2015
796.6—d23

Manufactured in the United States of America

CPSIA Compliance Information: Batch #CW15PK: For Further Information contact Rosen Publishing, New York, New York at 1-800-237-9932

CONTENIDO

CONTENTS

¿Tienes una patineta? Es muy divertido ir de un lugar a otro en patineta.

Do you have a scooter?
A scooter is a fun way to get from place to place.

La puedes montar solo.
También puedes ir
con tus amigos.

You can ride one by yourself.
You can also ride one
with your friends.

La mayoría de las patinetas se impulsa con el pie.

Most scooters are called kick scooters. You move them with your feet.

Para montar patineta hay que pararse en la **plataforma**. La plataforma es larga y plana.

Scooter riders stand on the **deck**. The deck is long and flat.

Las ruedas de la patineta
están cerca de tus pies.

Scooter wheels are
near your feet.

Algunas patinetas tienen dos ruedas. ¡Otras tienen tres o cuatro ruedas!

Some scooters have two wheels. Other scooters have three or four wheels!

Las patinetas pueden moverse muy rápido. Se puede disminuir la velocidad usando el freno.

Scooters can move fast. Riders slow down by using the brake.

el freno/ brake

A algunos les gusta hacer trucos. Saltar con toda la patineta se llama un salto del conejo.

Some riders like to do tricks. Jumping with the whole scooter is called a bunny hop.

El truco de **manual** es en el que se usa solo la rueda de atrás.

A **manual** is a trick where a rider uses only the back wheel.

Montar patineta es muy divertido. ¡Recuerda de siempre usar un casco!

Riding a scooter is a lot of fun. Remember to wear a helmet!

PALABRAS QUE DEBES SABER / WORDS TO KNOW

(la) plataforma/
deck

(el) manual/
manual

ÍNDICE / INDEX

SITIOS DE INTERNET / WEBSITES

Due to the changing nature of Internet links, PowerKids Press has developed an online list of websites related to the subject of this book. This site is updated regularly. Please use this link to access the list: www.powerkidslinks.com/wmg/scoo